SYLVIA PANKHURST

This book is from a series about Modern Women Artists
published by Eiderdown Books.

Other titles available from the same series:

To order books, please visit eiderdownbooks.com

SYLVIA PANKHURST

Katy Norris

EIDERDOWN
BOOKS

MODERN WOMEN ARTISTS

1. Studio portrait of Sylvia Pankhurst by Lena Connell, c.1906

As a modern artist, Sylvia Pankhurst (1882–1960) was unusual because her feminist views were inseparable from her practice. Alongside her efforts to become a professional painter and designer during the opening decade of the twentieth century, she was a high profile campaigner for the right to vote for women, a cause for which she devised a range of banners, jewellery designs and graphic logos. Most famously, Pankhurst worked for the Women's Social and Political Union (WSPU), the radical party of suffragettes founded by her mother Emmeline and sister Christabel, whose strategies of stone-throwing, window-smashing and even arson, have been historically cited as the defining aspects of the modern women's movement. Pankhurst was herself incarcerated for her role in this militant activism, although she questioned and increasingly disagreed with the WSPU's 'terrorist' tactics.[1] She experienced hunger striking and forcible feeding, expressing solidarity with her fellow political prisoners in one of her best-known designs, the *Holloway Brooch* (Fig. 2). Meanwhile, her trumpeting 'angel of freedom' emblem had broader appeal across the suffrage movement and became a popular motif for the entire campaign (see Fig. 27). Printed on everything from banners and political pamphlets to cups and saucers, it represented a powerful symbol of female expression and strength at a time when women were locked out of political debate.

This involvement in the campaign for female suffrage was informed by Pankhurst's strong socialist ideology. Her position was deeply personal, shaped by her upbringing in the

2. *Holloway Brooch*, c.1909, silver and enamel

cosmopolitan centres of Manchester and London during the 1880s and 1890s alongside the left-wing politics of Emmeline and her father Richard, both key supporters of the emergent labour movement in Britain. Pankhurst's ongoing commitment to improving the lives of the many rather than the privileged few differentiates her from Christabel and Emmeline, who moved increasingly to the right, as pressure mounted over the issue of enfranchisement. Whereas they fought to secure women's voting rights on the same terms as men – one third of whom were also disenfranchised – she supported the concept of universal suffrage and the entitlement of all citizens to vote, regardless of sex, class or property ownership. Pankhurst's belief that female emancipation was not just dependent on the vote, but on wider social reform too, inspired her to create 'Women Workers of England' in 1907 (Fig. 3), a series that provided a visual record of the arduous working lives of British women in industrial and agricultural communities. She gained publicity for the women's plight when her paintings were printed alongside an article published in *The London Magazine* in 1908, in which she argued for better labour conditions and greater parity between men and women's salaries.

Seen together, Pankhurst's suffrage designs and the 'Women Workers of England' series have huge resonance with today's discourses on gender equality – from the censorship of women and their right to freedom of expression, to the gender pay gap. Nevertheless, the relative obscurity of her images reveals a deficit in the accepted trajectory of modern art history. The proscriptive terms of Formalism – that is the theory that a picture's moral, social or narrative content should be secondary to its use of line, shape and colour – has dominated our understanding of twentieth-century art, determining which artists are upheld as paragons of their age and those who are simply dismissed or ignored.

Pankhurst exemplifies a category of forgotten 'women artists' who not only used their creative talent to draw attention

WOMEN · WORKERS ·
OF
ENGLAND
WRITTEN · AND · ILLUSTRATED · FROM · PAINTINGS
BY
SYLVIA · PANKHURST

THE BOOTMAKER.

SHE WORKS WITH AN ORDINARY TREADLE MACHINE, AND USUALLY CARRIES THE WORK RIGHT THROUGH FROM THE TIME THE DIFFERENT PARTS OF THE LEATHER AND LINING HAVE BEEN CUT OUT UNTIL THE SHOES ARE READY TO BE PLOUGHED AND TO HAVE THE SOLES FASTENED ON.

(299)

Y ·

3. 'Women Workers of England', from *The London Magazine*, 1907

to the struggle for women's rights, but typically worked in mediums other than oil painting and sculpture, employing their skills in textiles, print-making, sign-painting, jewellery design and illustration.[2] Unlike the canon of predominantly male artists who have been celebrated over the last century, these women did not typically produce a vast oeuvre of pictures to be sold in commercial galleries or exhibited in museums. Rather they were responsible for the formation of a new visual culture for the modern women's movement, a powerful form of 'political spectacle' designed to galvanise consensus on issues affecting the female population's everyday experience.[3]

This is not to say that the marriage of art and politics was without difficulty. In her personal account of the suffrage campaign published in 1931, Pankhurst summarised the disjunction between the 'purely egotistical struggle of the artist' and the collective endeavours of the activist driven by social conscience.[4] As she became ever more embroiled in political protest, Pankhurst experienced an increasing sense of futility towards her artistic vocation. 'As a speaker, a pamphlet-seller, a chalker of pavements, a canvasser on doorsteps you are wanted,' she exclaimed, 'as an artist the world has no real use for you'.[5] Eventually she came to the conclusion that these two aspects of her life were completely incompatible. 'Mothers came to me with their wasted little ones. I saw starvation look at me from patient eyes. I knew that I should never return to my art.'[6]

It is widely stated that Pankhurst had all but abandoned her artistic career by 1912, when she threw herself entirely into political activism. Undoubtedly the time she operated as a professional artist was short-lived, yet she continued to exercise her creativity in a number of literary projects, including her poetry and non-fiction writings and her editorial work for political newspapers such as the *Woman's Dreadnought* (later retitled *Worker's Dreadnought*). This publication was the official journalistic organ for her own suffragette party – the East

London Federation of Suffragettes (ELFS) – founded in 1914. While the importance of Pankhurst's input into the suffrage campaign requires further attention, the nature of this expansive creative outlook, shaped by a mind that was constantly politically and artistically engaged, also demands greater appreciation.[7] This publication seeks to explain the significant contribution that Pankhurst made to a turbulent era of modern British history, exploring how she forged a vital bridge between art, life and politics during a period of immense social upheaval.

An Education in Art and Politics: the Forming of Social Consciousness

From an early age, Pankhurst harboured an ambition to become 'a painter and draughtsman in the service of the great movements for social betterment'.[8] She developed her technical skills through her studies at the Manchester School of Art (1900–2) and then the Royal College of Art in London (1904–6), but it was before this, as a young girl growing up with politically active parents, that she first conceived that her talent for drawing could be utilised for a greater social purpose.

The Pankhurst home was indeed a space for cultural as well as political enlightenment. Both Richard and Emmeline Pankhurst were active members of the newly formed Independent Labour Party (ILP) and supported a range of dissident ideas, including universal suffrage for men and women. Socialism permeated their household in the form of regular political meetings attended by an eclectic mix of radicals, atheists, social reformers and revolutionaries, such as the ILP leader Keir Hardie (Fig. 4), the Russian communist Peter Kropotkin, the American slavery abolitionist William Lloyd Garrison, the women's rights activist Annie Besant and the Arts and Crafts designer and anarchist

4. *Keir Hardie*, c.1910, watercolour on paper

William Morris. To some extent the Pankhursts seemed to share Morris' disdain for new industrial processes, believing like him in the return to hand-craftsmanship as a route to a fairer and more equal society. In the mid-1890s, Emmeline Pankhurst opened Emerson & Co., a home decoration shop specialising in hand-made goods, which was progressive in terms of how it placed women, both as pioneering decorators within the home and entrepreneurial business people. The company provided an early outlet for Sylvia's creativity, presenting the opportunity to design products such as patterned plates, vases and folding screens. Nevertheless, her primary intention was to create decorative work that had wider social reach, a desire that only intensified with the loss of her father at the age of just 16.

In this regard, the influence of another leading Arts and Crafts proponent, Walter Crane, was crucial. Crane was a commanding figure in late-nineteenth-century culture – a political cartoonist and children's book illustrator, as well as a respected artist–craftsman and educator in the field of design. It is often said that he invented the iconography of British socialism, since his pictures – a blend of industrial, agricultural and artistic imagery infused with allegorical emblems such as goddesses and sphynxes – saturated the labour press and were taken up by trade unions for their banner logos and designs.[9] Pankhurst had been exposed to his work from a young age in the form of his popular Routledge Toy Books, as well as his widely celebrated *The Triumph of Labour* (1891), a ubiquitous socialist illustration featuring a woman in the guise of the 'angel of freedom' leading the triumphant procession of workers. With these artistic endeavours, Crane hoped to engender what might be described as visual literacy: an active and critical mode of reading images that guided interpreters – adults and children alike – in recognising and resisting the corrupting influences of capitalism. He argued that art was simply a form of writing, and that design in particular constituted a common language that could communicate complex concepts in more relatable terms. In his hands, ornamental elements functioned much like printed words, explicating his political ideology with easily recognisable symbols that could be universally understood regardless of age, gender or class.

Such ideas and strategies were the basis for a lecture on ornament and design delivered by Crane in 1902 at the Manchester School of Art, where Pankhurst, as a young art student, enthusiastically received his teachings. It was around this time that she began to envisage how her artworks might bring about a higher level of political consciousness. 'I would ... portray the world that is to be when poverty is no more,' she determined. 'I would decorate halls where people would foregather in the movement to win the new world, and make banners for meetings and processions.'[10] In these aspirations, Pankhurst was, like Crane, motivated by a desire for a world of greater equality and opportunity. However, as her individual political ideology evolved she went on to use her creative talents primarily for the purpose of promoting women's rights, adapting and expanding Crane's socialist iconography for the suffrage cause.

The opportunity to develop her skills in the art of wall-painting and decoration arose when Pankhurst was awarded the highly sought-after Proctor Travelling Studentship – also in 1902 – a grant that enabled her to take up residency abroad for the purpose of furthering her artistic training. Initially she planned to divide her time between studying mosaics in Venice and frescos in Florence although, as events transpired, she found much to occupy herself in Venice and remained in the city for the entirety of the placement. Pankhurst fell into a demanding yet productive routine, working through from 5am until 8pm. In the early mornings and afternoons, she painted outdoors, making scenes of Venetian street life. During the height of the day she took shelter from the Mediterranean sun, copying examples of decorative art in Venice's many churches and civic buildings. In the winter of

5. (opposite) Study of interior mosaics of St Mark's Basilica, 1902, watercolour and ink on paper **6.** (above) Study of interior mosaics of St Mark's Basilica, 1902, watercolour, ink and gold paint on paper

1902, she enrolled at the prestigious *Accademia di Belle Arti*, where she overcame institutional barriers by being the only woman in her cohort to join a life drawing class studying the nude model.

Having previously travelled little outside her homes in Manchester and London, Pankhurst relished her new cultural environment and the opportunity of studying historic works of art *in situ*. She later noted that her surroundings in Venice were filled with 'peace and beauty', a comment that resonates particularly with her artistic interpretation of the immersive atmosphere of St Mark's cathedral.[11] Pankhurst responded to the cycle of Byzantine mosaics that adorned this immense structure, with its curving domes and vaults, as a shimmering, active presence. One study of the cathedral's icons, a portrait of St Theodore, reveals how she made every effort to represent the hundreds of small coloured glass tiles that comprised the saint's face, skin and hair, while simultaneously catching the play of light upon the gold surface, using fluid brushstrokes and careful modulations of tone and colour (Fig. 5). Her copy of the biblical narrative scene *Angel at the Tomb of Christ* – a dominant motif in the cathedral, located between its nave and central cupola – is looser still in its handling (Fig. 6). This time the painting is executed imaginatively, with sketchy touches of gold paint that bring a warm tonality to the picture and a sense of movement, as though seen under flickering candle light. Pankhurst's interpretation of these subjects suggest that she was not only interested in imitating the flattened style of early Christian iconography – itself a highly effective form of symbolic language used for religious rather than political instruction – but also in capturing something of her experiential encounter with the mosaics within the spatial and atmospheric conditions in St Mark's. The exercise apparently provided an important lesson in public decoration that would inform her suffrage art, causing her to consider not just the emblematic impact of her images but also how their particular placement in public settings might engage her audience both physically and emotionally.

It was this interest in site-specific public art that attracted Pankhurst to another historic building, the *Scuola di San Giorgio degli Schiavoni* and its cycle of large-scale paintings by the Renaissance painter Vittore Carpaccio. Traditionally, *scuole* (or 'schools' in Italian) played an important civic role in Venice, functioning as meeting places for confraternities that drew from a broad base of society, including men and women from all levels of social and economic class. Still active during the early 1900s, the 'degli Schiavoni', as it was commonly known, served the interests of artisans and working-class fishing communities and was decorated by Carpaccio's scenes celebrating the inspirational lives of the *scuole*'s patron saints. Pankhurst turned her attention to elements of pageantry in Carpaccio's depiction of the legend of St George and the Dragon. She copied details from one picture, in which the hero is welcomed home after slaying his ferocious adversary, with a celebratory procession complete with a stately king and princess mounted upon white horses.

Similar displays of medieval heraldry were to become an important theme in suffrage iconography, though it is perhaps surprising that Pankhurst was attracted to these types of hierarchic ceremony, given her socialist beliefs. It seems however, that for her, such narratives represented a vital means of escapism. The communal meeting house of the *Scuola di San Giorgio degli Schiavoni* – much like the sacred space of St Mark's basilica – occupied an idealised, heavenly, place in her mind. It was a small glimmer of the 'new world' that she and her fellow activists were hoping to establish by joining together and overturning social exploitation and inequality. In this sense it seems appropriate that while a large part of Pankhurst's placement in Venice was dedicated to copying pictures of divine saints and miraculous events, she also immersed herself in everyday life, making observational watercolour sketches and oil paintings of ordinary street scenes (Fig. 7). During her time in the Italian city, the two strands of her aesthetic emerged: the realist style that she used to highlight the plight of the most impoverished members of society, and a potent symbolism deriving from the Art and Crafts tradition with which she communicated her powerful vision for a better world.

In the first instance it was the latter style that Pankhurst had cause to draw upon. On her return to Manchester in 1903 she was commissioned to create a decorative scheme for a new meeting house that the ILP was building in Salford in memory of Richard Pankhurst. Although the project inevitably had huge personal significance, Pankhurst approached the task with considerable professionalism. Within three months she had diligently devised a scheme for the building's entrance inscribed with the motto 'England arise', and a large lecture hall comprised of iconography that reflected both the Labour party's founding principles and her personal admiration for her father. As a promotional exercise, Pankhurst had an explanation of the symbolic scheme printed upon cards headed with her studio address: 'As this hall bears the name of a pioneer whose life was given for the ideal and for the future, emblems of the future and the ideal have been chosen with which to decorate it ... Roses – love, apple trees – knowledge, doves – peace, corn – plenty, lilies – purity, honesty – honesty, bees – industry, sunflower and butterflies – hope.'[12]

The cards were handed out during an inauguration ceremony introduced by Walter Crane, at which Pankhurst also gave a presentation. In this moment the socialist underpinnings of her childhood, her ambition to carve her way as a professional artist and the flowering of her own radical political consciousness drew neatly together. Yet there was a discrepancy in the project that could not be overlooked. The branch of the ILP in Salford, for which Pankhurst Hall was

7. *Venetian Street Scene*, 1902, watercolour on paper

conceived, functioned as a social club for men only – a fact that caused outrage amongst the female members of the Pankhurst family. From this episode, Emmeline and Christabel went on to establish a new women's organisation, the WSPU, which could focus squarely on establishing women's rights. Sylvia Pankhurst meanwhile spent much of her early adulthood trying to reconcile this troubling anomaly in the ILP's constitution. As her art demonstrates she never lost sight of the intrinsic link between class and gender when fighting for social justice, attempting at every opportunity to build a better alliance between the values of the labour movement and the women's movement.

Registering and Recording Women's Experiences

In 1905 Pankhurst created two near identical postcard designs for the ILP and WSPU that can be categorised as early attempts at visual propaganda. The first, commissioned by Keir Hardie in support of the ILP's proposal for a new parliamentary unemployment bill, drew attention to the plight of out-of-work labourers, featuring a crowd of protestors demanding the vote (Fig. 8). In the foreground a woman and man, both with thick-set features and dressed in labourer's clothes, stand together grasping a placard pronouncing, 'Workless and Hungry. Vote for the Bill.' While in this picture both genders are given equal representation, in the second image, this time created for the WSPU's membership card, an all-female group takes centre stage (Fig. 9). The man in the foreground has been replaced by a woman defiantly holding aloft a large banner that simply reads: 'VOTES, VOTES, VOTES', while beside her now stands a figure holding a baby. The image not only functioned broadly as a call to arms to working-class women, but also highlighted the predicament of mothers forced to support their families on unequal and tokenistic wages. This subject was addressed more explicitly in a third design, the poetically entitled, *Feed My*

Lambs (Fig. 10), in which a woman appears against a pastoral backdrop, her head bowed in quiet contemplation, as she embraces her two children drinking from a pitcher of milk.

The emotive appeal of *Feed My Lambs*, coupled with the timeless and elegiac representation of a mother and her children, seems passive when compared with the vigorous demands for the vote represented in the ILP and WSPU postcards. Nevertheless, in this and the ILP design the use of bold outlines, reminiscent of a heavy woodcut technique, effectively evokes a sense of immediacy and primitivism that can be associated with a grass-roots uprising. All three images place the needs of working-class women at the centre of their demand for political change, making a link between social betterment and universal enfranchisement. The condition of these women was 'indeed terrible', Pankhurst declared. 'Who can fail to connect this with their unfranchised state?' she asked.[13]

Little sympathy for her concerns could be found in the policies of the ILP or WSPU. The majority of the Labour party did not wish to fight for women's votes for fear that this might hinder its chances of securing the same right for working-class men. Meanwhile the WSPU considered the enfranchisement of working-class women a leap too far for the British political establishment, and concentrated their campaign instead on securing voting rights for the upper and middle-classes. There was further disparity between Pankhurst and the WSPU leadership that highlights the radical, wide-reaching reforms she was seeking. In her endeavour to form an effective, single-issue pressure group, Christabel rejected anything that threatened to divert attention away from female enfranchisement. For this reason, she frequently overlooked evidence of women's vulnerabilities, preferring to present her followers in the WSPU as an 'army' that was primed and ready to take a decisive role in political life. Sylvia Pankhurst, by contrast, was much more willing to show the structural imbalances within society that were keeping women in a weakened or

8. *Workless and Hungry. Vote for the Bill*, 1906, print on card

9. WSPU Member's Card, 1906, print on card

10. *Feed My Lambs*, c.1906, ink on paper

11. 'What It Feels Like To Be In Prison', from the *Pall Mall Magazine*, May 1908

impoverished position. Her art was intended to register the socioeconomic as well as political disadvantages faced by women, and to raise awareness of aspects of their lives where they were most at risk of discrimination.

This difference in attitude can be demonstrated by the way in which the two sisters viewed the imprisonment of suffragettes. Whereas Christabel saw the issue in terms of political gain, enthusiastically portraying WSPU prisoners as heroic martyrs willing to suffer for the suffrage cause, Sylvia Pankhurst immediately identified injustice in how women were treated by the penal system. This applied, she argued, not just to female protesters, incarcerated for their role in political activism, but ordinary prisoners typically deriving from working-class backgrounds. Some five years before the government's Cat and Mouse Act made the dilemma of detaining suffragettes a national issue – by which time a dangerous pattern of hunger striking and forcible feeding had developed – Pankhurst expressed her concerns in 'What It Feels Like to be in Prison' (1907).[14] This was a first-hand account of gruelling prison life based upon her time at Holloway prison after she was jailed for WSPU activity in 1906.

The article was published in the *Pall Mall Magazine* and illustrated by Pankhurst using simple black and white line drawings each representing a woman acting out different prison routines (Fig. 11). There is an almost childlike literalness about the way she arranged the pictures in a quarter-page format, divided by a linear grid reminiscent of prison bars. The images are accompanied by banners reading 'Ready for Supper', 'Scrubbing the Bed', 'Dinner' and 'The Breakfast Basket' which help to build a concrete understanding of the women's experience in the mind of the viewer. The informative nature of these pictures contrasts dramatically with a wistful portrait that Pankhurst made of herself dressed in prison clothes (Fig. 12). In this pastel and charcoal drawing, an ethereal quality is created by delicate smudging and blending around

12. *Self-portrait*, c.1907, pastel and charcoal on paper

the artist's face, yet the illusion is broken towards the bottom of the picture, where Pankhurst's handling descends into broad, gestural strokes. It is perhaps understandable that a work produced in prison should be left incomplete, however in this instance the sketchy finish feels deliberate, as though Pankhurst was hoping to imprint something of her own immense physical and mental struggle upon the picture. The technique appears in a second self-portrait, as well as a further related drawing, both of which feature young women wearing the same worker's sunbonnets (Figs 13–14). Again, Pankhurst created a strong impression of her sitters as embodied subjects, evoking through her sensitive portrayal of the women's characterful expressions, pale complexions and flushed cheeks an overwhelming sense of their physical and psychological presence.

Meanwhile Pankhurst found new ways to communicate her outrage at the trauma inflicted on female prisoners. In 1913, another testimonial, *Forcibly-Fed*, appeared in the American current-affairs journal, *McClure's Magazine* in which she recalled the brutal and invasive procedure of force-feeding:

> I felt a man's hands trying to force my mouth open. I set my teeth and tightened my lips over them with all my strength. My breath was coming so quickly that I felt as if I should suffocate. I felt his fingers trying to press my lips apart, – getting inside, – and I felt them and a steel gag running around my gums and feeling for gaps in my teeth ... infinitely worse than any pain was the sense of degradation, the sense that the very fight that one made against the repeated outrage was shattering one's nerves and breaking down one's control.[15]

In its use of violent and sexualised language, this account differs again from the informative tone of 'What it Feels Like to be in Prison' and yet, in all of Pankhurst's writings and imagery relating to prison life, she was guided by her motivation to convey women's visceral responses to the ordeal of incarceration.

13. *Self-portrait*, *c.*1907–10, chalk on paper

14. *Portrait of a Young Woman*, c.1910, chalk on paper

Above all, Pankhurst's literary and visual talents came together most effectively in 'Women Workers of England'.[16] The series consists of gouache paintings, as well as a small group of charcoal drawings (Figs 15–21), that were originally published together alongside a dedicated article in *The London Magazine* in November 1908, and then individually in the WSPU journal *Votes for Women* between 1908 and 1911. For this task Pankhurst immersed herself fully in the lives of her subjects, painting and writing about female labourers, their working conditions and processes of production, all the while residing in the communities she studied. Much of her early campaigning had concentrated on the cosmopolitan centre of London. Now she travelled across the industrial north of England and Scotland to meet women in Cradley Heath, Stoke-on-Trent, Wigan, Leicester, Scarborough, Berwick-upon-Tweed and Glasgow, building affiliations with suffrage groups that were linked to reformist trade union groups interested specifically in worker's rights.

Pankhurst chose to depict a diverse range of industries, including boot-making, coalmining, chain-making, fishing, farming and cotton-spinning. At every turn she noted female employees' long hours and low wages, always unequal to the men they worked alongside. The problems were most acute in the Staffordshire potteries, where women were often limited to unskilled labour, assisting men in their more specialist and highly paid productions. 'A woman was turning the wheel for the thrower, a woman was treading the lathe for the turner,' Pankhurst recounted: 'each was employed by the man she toiled for – the slave of a slave, I thought!'[17] There were issues too with dangerous equipment and materials. With the exception of Wedgwood pottery, manufacturers in Staffordshire used a lead glaze that caused stillborn births, paralysis and colic amongst its female workforce, while the waste products generated by cotton mills in Glasgow frequently resulted in employees developing respiratory diseases. Overall,

15. 'The Chainmaker', from *The London Magazine*, 1908

16. *Untitled (Women working at benches in a shoemaking factory)*, 1907, gouache on paper

17. (above) *An Old-fashioned Pottery Turning
Jasper Ware,* 1907, gouache on paper **18.** (opposite) *In a Glasgow Cotton
Spinning Mill: Changing the Bobbin,* 1907, gouache on paper

19. (opposite) *Old Fashioned Pottery: Transferring the pattern onto the biscuit*, 1907, bodycolour **20.** (above) *Scotch Fisher Lassie Cutting Herrings*, 1907, gouache on paper

Pankhurst noted that women who worked in agricultural roles were healthier than their sisters in the factories, since they had constant access to fresh air and necessarily developed stronger physiques.

As an artist Pankhurst made some personal identifications with the working women she portrayed. Like them, she was involved in a form of production, yet she recognised an important difference between creative methods that could be considered craftwork, and types of labour that had undergone a process of industrialisation. In Leicester she expressed a degree of empathy with self-employed women who made boots at home and created every part themselves, compared to factory workers who were responsible for one piece of a larger production line. 'As the women working there rose from their monotonous task, repeating year in year out the same operation, perhaps machining toe-caps – always toe-caps, they would crowd around my easel full of interest. I was astonished by their oft-repeated comment: "I should never have the patience to do it!"'[18]

Such commentary highlights the psychological distance between the Leicester boot-makers and Pankhurst, who, as an educated, middle-class woman, inhabited an entirely different social position to the working-class women she encountered. In her paintings too, this sense of detachment prevails. Pankhurst's subjects tend to be represented in a state of absorption, with their heads bowed in concentration, intensely focused on their work, or else staring vaguely into the middle distance as though entirely closed off from the scrutinising gaze of the observer. Their remoteness is confounded by Pankhurst's cool palette and controlled technical execution, with which, in keeping with realist traditions, she also paid careful attention to intricate details of surfaces, equipment and materials. There are some exceptions in her group of

21. *Dipping and Drying on the Mangle*, 1907, charcoal and gouache on paper

charcoal drawings, which demonstrate a more expressive approach. In *Dipping and Drying on the Mangle* (Fig. 21), for example, Pankhurst dispensed with the smooth finish that distinguished her watercolours, creating instead deliberate blotches and stains of white gouache on the surface of the paper that are suggestive of clay splashes from the workers' machinery. The technique has the effect of bringing the world of the factory closer to the viewer.

Pankhurst's handling of this working-class subject matter links her to other female artists committed to producing socially engaging art, most notably the German printmaker Käthe Kollwitz, whose print cycles *The Weaver's Revolt* (1898) and *The Peasant's War* (1908) were familiar amongst artistic circles in Britain during the early 1900s. Both artists bought their socialist feminist ideologies to bear on their representations of working women, using their art to highlight the intolerable conditions forced upon the poor. It is worth noting that compared to Kollwitz's peasants, which appear as generic, proletariat masses, Pankhurst afforded her subjects more individuality, particularly in single portraits, as can be seen in the two Glasgow pictures *Changing the Bobbin* (see Fig. 18) and *Minding a Pair of Fine Frames* (reproduced on the front cover of this book) wherein distinct personalities and characteristics begin to emerge. It is also true however, that Kollwitz's peasants are empowered to rise up against their oppressors, whereas the female workers in Pankhurst's series are entirely subordinated by their social circumstances. Rather than addressing the working-class women she studied, Pankhurst directed her writings and imagery at the middle-class readership of *The London Magazine* and *Votes For Women*. In doing so she raised awareness of the dire situation experienced by the lower classes, but she also afforded them little agency to improve their condition for themselves.

These difficulties offer possible reasons why Pankhurst herself grew frustrated with her artistic practice. From 1912 onwards, she elected to commit herself entirely to political activism in order to achieve social reform. In 1914 she set about mobilising one of the country's poorest communities when she founded the ELFS, for which she organised public meetings, opened women's social centres and produced a weekly newspaper, the *Woman's Dreadnought*. In the meantime, however, she channelled her energies into the WSPU's campaign for suffrage, returning to the symbolic language and immersive decorative schemes that she had envisaged as a young art student.

The Art of Protest

In her influential study of suffragist art, the art historian Lisa Tickner identifies certain limitations to Pankhurst's creative contribution to the campaign. She argues that the switch Pankhurst made from the Social Realist style of the WSPU membership card, to the agricultural and biblical allegory seen in emblems such as the 'angel of freedom', was the 'pictorial equivalent of the heightened religiose rhetoric' used by the WSPU to consolidate the power of its middle and upper classes leaders.[19] According to Tickner, pastoral and religious symbolism laden with idealised images of women ultimately served to weaken Pankhurst's case for social and political reform, since it was steeped in the very kind of backwards traditions from which she was trying to break free.

More recently academics specialising in women's art have sought to reframe this argument. Rosemary Betterton, for example, attempts to show how the language of symbolism, with its ability to unlock internal experience and emotion through universal signifiers, emerged as an effective vehicle for self-expression amongst women who were experiencing 'a changing sense of themselves as political subjects' during the early twentieth century.[20] She discusses Pankhurst's allegorical imagery in terms of the 'cyclical and monumental over the social-historical', referencing the writings of the feminist philosopher Julia Kristeva to explain why the artist did not take up either Social Realism or emerging forms of Modernist abstraction in her demand for female suffrage. According to this analysis, female artists and designers such as Pankhurst intentionally refused the latest developments in aesthetic style, instead preferring traditional religious and historic iconography that had provided strong cultural referents for womanhood through the ages.

Certainly, familiar stereotypes of femininity that emphasised women's spiritual purity or their inherent place within the natural world provided suffragists with a sense of rootedness and stability that was, as Tickner points out, particularly appealing to conventional middle-class supporters. The methods used by protesters to disseminate their symbolic iconography were, nevertheless, radical and were designed to target all levels of society. Amongst the most significant developments for the women's movement was the technical advancement of printing processes, namely colour lithography, which allowed campaigners to reproduce eye-catching emblems on a range of commercial and political products. Typically, Pankhurst's designs for the WSPU were printed in the party's official colours – purple, white and green, symbolising dignity, purity and hope – and figured on ephemera as diverse as packaging, greetings cards, posters, pamphlets, badges, and crockery.

It is through these items that we can trace the evolution of Pankhurst's 'angel of freedom' motif, the earliest manifestation of which emerged around 1908 and appeared on many artefacts, including the first bound volume of *Votes for Women* and an official WSPU tea set (Fig. 22). The image consists of a left-facing winged angel set against a circular purple and green background. The figure places a trumpet to her lips, apparently announcing news of the fledgling suffragette movement, while behind her a banner flutters, inscribed with the word 'freedom'. Pankhurst's inclusion of prison bars and

22. (top) HM Williamson & Sons, WSPU tea set, *c.*1909, bone china with printed transfers **23.** (above) Misses MA and E. Brice, West Ham WSPU Banner replicating trumpeting angel motif, 1909–10, cotton, silk, metal and card

chains alongside this otherwise spiritual symbolism underlined the WSPU's militancy. This was a characteristic that defined the suffragettes from the more moderate suffragists, and communicated the party's core belief that emancipation could only come from violent struggle and personal sacrifice.

The 'angel of freedom' was taken up widely by WSPU members, including the party's West Ham branch which adapted the emblem for a silk banner inscribed with the words 'COURAGE CONSTANCY SUCCESS' (Fig. 23). Meanwhile Pankhurst made a number of adaptations from her initial design. Continuing the prison theme, Pankhurst incorporated trumpeting angels in her design for an illuminated address that was received by suffragette prisoners in recognition of their bravery and commitment to the cause (Fig. 24). A WSPU calendar produced in 1910 represents a winged angel on its cover, this time showing her holding up a candle to guide the path of a suffragette dressed in prison garb and carrying a folded 'Votes for Women' banner over her shoulder (Fig. 25). Another variation that was reproduced on a tin badge featured a now wingless angel facing forward as she breaks through the prison bars, a flock of doves flying out from the cell behind her (Fig. 26).

Just as modern printing techniques played a significant role in the aesthetic of the suffrage campaign, traditional forms of craft such as jewellery design and banner-making found their place in this new visual culture of protest. For suffrage artists, the politicising possibilities of these hand-held objects was huge, since their tangibility allowed individuals to forge physical attachments to the ideals of the campaign. Pankhurst astutely understood that the experience of holding a banner aloft in a procession or rally alongside fellow comrades evoked an embodied sense of the suffragette's shared aims and interests. She is known to have created at least five stand-alone

24. Illuminated Scroll Presented to Holloway Prisoners by the WSPU, c.1909, print on paper

To Elsa Gye.

On behalf of all women who will win freedom by the bondage which you have endured for their sake, and dignity by the humiliation which you have gladly suffered for the uplifting of our sex. We, the Members of the Women's Social and Political Union, herewith express our deep sense of admiration for your courage in enduring a long period of privation and solitary confinement in prison for the Votes for Women Cause, also our thanks to you for the great service that you have thereby rendered to the Woman's Movement. Inspired by your passion for freedom and right may we and the women who come after us be ever ready to follow your example of self-forgetfulness and self conquest, ever ready to obey the call of duty and to answer to the appeal of the oppressed.

Signed on behalf of the Women's Social and Political Union.

A VOTES FOR WOMEN CALENDAR·

19 10.

W S

P U.

25. (opposite) WSPU calendar, 1910, print on card
26. (top) WSPU badge, 1908, tin badge
27. (above) Angel of Freedom emblem, 1908, print on paper

protest banners for the WSPU, which carried both personal messages of identification and broad statements of camaraderie. One repeated the WSPU's strategy of achieving the vote through sacrifice – this time through the symbolism of a pelican piercing its breast to feed its young. Another, a green banner bordered by a thick purple margin featuring gold lettering encompassed by floral wreaths, reflected Pankhurst's own socialist feminist ideology in the statement 'Human Emancipation must precede Social Regeneration'.

Items of jewellery were similarly instrumental in bridging the separation between individual and collective experience, since they functioned both as personal keepsakes and sartorial items for display. This is best exemplified by Pankhurst's *Holloway Brooch* (see Fig. 2), awarded, like the illuminated address, to all WSPU detainees upon their release from prison. Composed of silver with coloured enamel embellishment, the design cleverly welded together the portcullis icon of the House of Commons with the broad arrow symbol routinely used on British prison uniforms during the period. The brooch's strong graphic combination came to stand as a potent symbol of female solidarity as well as a personal souvenir of members' involvement in the campaign.

Pankhurst's most ambitious contribution to the campaign came when the WSPU staged its *Women's Exhibition* at the Prince's Skating Rink in London in 1909 (Figs 28–9). The event took the idea of the political occupation of space beyond the familiar bounds of street protest, presenting a populist educational exhibit complete with replica prison cells, a mock polling booth and cartoon models of suffragette deputations. Pankhurst devised the entire decorative scheme, focusing her efforts on an immense cycle of site-specific banners. The chief compositions, painted upon huge strips of canvas, were placed at either end of the hall and bore representations of idealised female agricultural labourers dressed in arcadian robes and flanked by flowering almond trees and angels. Along the sides

28. Christina Broom, WSPU *Women's Exhibition* featuring Sylvia Pankhurst's decorative mural scheme, 1909, glassplate photograph

29. WSPU *Women's Exhibition* featuring Sylvia Pankhurst's
decorative mural scheme, 1909, photograph

of the hall, Pankhurst placed a dynamic sequence of icons: a gilded prison arrow symbolising struggle, a pelican feeding its young for sacrifice and an olive branch for pacifism. While the two end pictures communicated her vision for a more equal, peaceful and prosperous world, this iconography provided instruction on how such a realm might be reached. A clue was given in a biblical extract, incorporated into the image on the backwall and seen by visitors as they exited the hall: 'They that sow in tears shall reap in joy. He that goeth and weepeth, bearing precious seed, shall doubtless come again with rejoicing, bringing his sheaves with him.' In these words and images, the WSPU's tenet of salvation through sacrifice was again extolled, but so too was Pankhurst's personal vision of a utopian future – a pastoral ideal shaped by her socialist feminist ideology, which was dependent on peaceful compromise as much as violent struggle.

New Directions

Pankhurst's designs for the *Women's Exhibition* help to explain her growing ideological dissatisfaction with the WSPU. While she evidently held on to visions of a peaceful future bought about by a socialist alliance between the labour movement and the women's movement, Christabel and Emmeline were becoming ever more divisive. From 1912 they effectively ended the creative dimension of the WSPU's campaign when they redirected efforts away from political pageantry to hard-line agitation. Under this new phase of enhanced militancy, the WSPU advocated attacks on public art and architecture, a tactic against which Sylvia Pankhurst was unequivocally opposed. By 1914 differences had mounted irrevocably, leading her to split from the WSPU and form the ELFS.

Pankhurst's work for the ELFS saw her lobbying against inequalities that went far deeper than the single-issue of women's suffrage, setting in motion her enduring struggle against a range of social injustices including class discrimination, chauvinism, racism and imperialism. During the war she adopted a firm pacifist position and devoted herself to social welfare work, setting up a co-operative toy factory and a volunteer-run mother and baby clinic. When the Representation of the People Act was granted in 1918, Pankhurst objected to its 'absurd restrictions', which only gave voting rights to women aged over 30. This was an anomaly only overturned by the Equal Franchise Act of 1928 that finally gave women electoral parity with men.[21] Pankhurst, meanwhile, fervently supported the Soviet revolution and global communism. In the 1920s and 1930s she rallied against the rise of extreme right wing politics in Europe, particularly under the dictator Mussolini in Italy, which eventually led her to dedicate her life to the liberation of Ethiopia from Italian fascist rule.

Inevitably these causes absorbed much of Pankhurst's time and energy. Nevertheless, the literary work she produced over the decades following her full-time commitment to social activism shows that her artistic imagination never tired, even though her career as a painter and designer had officially ended. A volume of poetry authored soon after another stretch in Holloway prison in 1920, *Writ on Cold Slate*, exemplifies her artistic eye in the use of highly emotive and symbolic language, while the political cartoons that she selected to print as editor of the *Woman's Dreadnought* and *Workers' Dreadnought* demonstrate again her astute understanding for how radical political arguments could be translated into visually inspiring, agitational images.

This activity adds to our understanding of Pankhurst's diversity as a both a creative individual and a political icon. Indeed, it is just another example of how this extraordinary modern figure resisted easy categorisation. A prominent suffragette, her ideas differed from leading suffrage opinion, since she argued for a complete restructuring of the British socio-political system at a time when prominent figures, including Emmeline and Christabel Pankhurst, demanded merely to be admitted into the existing male political establishment. In her artistic career too, she refused to conform to expected patterns and trends. While stylistic innovation and Formalist abstraction have been earmarked as the defining characteristics of early twentieth-century art, Pankhurst was comfortable to move between established Realist and Symbolist aesthetics as her political agenda demanded. In this practice she was nonetheless ambitious and visionary, astutely exploiting developments in printed media and public decoration in order to bring together words, pictures and symbols that promoted understanding and raised awareness for her socialist feminist cause. Above all, by creating art for the popular domain rather than museums and galleries, she moved women's lives from the periphery to the centre, setting an important precedent for feminist artists and activists in the later part of the twentieth century.

Notes

1 Sylvia Pankhurst, 'The women's movement yesterday and today', undated, E. Sylvia Pankhurst papers (PP), no. 131, International Institute of Social History, Amsterdam.

2 Since the early 1970s there has been recognition of the lack of knowledge about the careers and artistic production of women, including a rich layering of feminist scholarship that ranges from the straight-forward question of neglect and projects of rediscovery to studies that penetrate more deeply into notions of power, representation and subjectivity. Since we do not speak of 'men artists' the very term 'women artists' has come to be understood as a troubled term, which highlights the rarity and marginalisation of female practitioners within the cannon of art history. See Griselda Pollock and Rozsika Parker (eds), *Old Mistresses: Women, Art and Ideology* (London 1981); Lisa Tickner, 'Feminism, Art History and Sexual Difference', *Genders* 3 (Fall 1988), pp.92–128; and Katy Deepwell (ed.), *Women Artists and Modernism* (Manchester 1998).

3 Lisa Tickner, *The Spectacle of Women* (London 1987).

4 Sylvia Pankhurst, *The Suffragette Movement – An Intimate Account of Persons and Ideals* (1931), p.218.

5 Pankhurst, quoted in Tickner (cited note 3), p.29.

6 Ibid.

7 This book builds on previous accounts of Pankhurst's art by Richard Pankhurst, *Sylvia Pankhurst: Artist and Crusader* (New York 1979); see also Hilary Cunliffe-Charlesworth, 'Sylvia Pankhurst as an Art Student' and Jackie Duckworth, 'Sylvia Pankhurst as an Artist', both included in Ian Bullock and Richard Pankhurst (eds), *Sylvia Pankhurst: From Artist to Anti-Fascist* (London 1992).

8 Pankhurst (cited note 4), p.104.

9 For more on Walter Crane see Morna O'Neil, *Walter Crane: The Arts and Crafts, Painting, and Politics 1875–1890* (London and New Haven 2010).

10 Sylvia Pankhurst in The Countess of Oxford and Asquith (ed.), *Myself When Young by Famous Women Today* (London 1938).

11 Pankhurst (cited note 7), p.161.

12 Quoted in Richard Pankhurst (cited note 7), p.40.

13 Sylvia Pankhurst, 'The chain makers of Cradley Heath', undated, PP no. 27.

14 The 1913 Cat and Mouse Act allowed for the early release of prisoners who were so weakened by hunger striking that they were at risk of death. They were to be recalled to prison once their health was recovered, where the process would begin again.

15 Sylvia Pankhurst, 'Forcibly Fed', *McClure's Magazine*, Aug 1913, pp.87–93.

16 For more on the 'Women Workers' series see Jacqueline Mulhallen, 'Sylvia Pankhurst's Paintings: A Missing Link', *Women's History Magazine*, Summer 2009.

17 Pankhurst (cited note 7), pp.262–4.

18 Ibid.

19 Lisa Tickner, *The Spectacle of Women* (London 1987).

20 Rosemary Betterton, 'Women artists, modernity and suffrage cultures in Britain and Germany 1890–1920', in Deepwell (cited note 2), pp.26–8.

21 Pankhurst (cited note 4), p.608.

Image credits

Cover: *In a Glasgow Cotton Mill: Minding a Pair of Fine Frames*, 1907, gouache on paper, 59 × 43.8 cm, private collection. Image courtesy Scarborough Museums Trust.

1. Studio portrait of Sylvia Pankhurst by Lena Connell, *c.*1906 © the estate of the artist. Image © Museum of London.
2. *Holloway Brooch*, *c.*1909, silver and enamel, H: 2 cm; L: 2.5 cm, Museum of London © Museum of London.
3. 'Women Workers of England', from *The London Magazine*, 1907, Lynx Theatre and Poetry.
4. *Keir Hardie*, *c.*1910, watercolour on paper, 37.7 × 26.8 cm, National Portrait Gallery, London © National Portrait Gallery, London.
5. Study of interior mosaics of St Mark's Basilica, 1902, watercolour and ink on paper, 49 × 30 cm, private collection. Image courtesy Lynx Theatre and Poetry.
6. Study of interior mosaics of St Mark's Basilica, 1902, watercolour, ink and gold paint on paper, 23 × 26 cm, private collection. Image courtesy Lynx Theatre and Poetry.
7. *Venetian Street Scene*, 1902, watercolour on paper, 43 × 27 cm, private collection. Image courtesy Lynx Theatre and Poetry.
8. *Workless and Hungry. Vote for the Bill*, 1906, print on card, dimensions unknown, Pankhurst collection, International Institute of Social History (Amsterdam).
9. WSPU Member's Card, 1906, print on card, H: 22.5 cm; W: 14.5 cm, private collection. Image courtesy Scarborough Museums Trust.
10. *Feed My Lambs*, *c.*1906, ink on paper, dimensions unknown, Pankhurst collection, International Institute of Social History (Amsterdam).
11. 'What It Feels Like To Be In Prison', the *Pall Mall Magazine*, May 1908, Pankhurst collection, International Institute of Social History (Amsterdam).
12. *Self-portrait*, *c.*1907, pastel and charcoal on paper, H: 66 cm; L: 56 cm (overall), Museum of London. Image © Helen Pankhurst/Museum of London.

13. *Self-portrait*, *c*.1907–10, chalk on paper, 66.3 × 51.1 cm, National Portrait Gallery, London. Image © National Portrait Gallery, London.

14. *Portrait of a Young Woman*, *c*.1910, chalk on paper, dimensions unknown, private collection. Image courtesy Scarborough Museums Trust.

15. 'The Chainmaker', from *The London Magazine*, 1908, Lynx Theatre and Poetry. Image courtesy Lynx Theatre and Poetry.

16. *Untitled (Women working at benches in a shoemaking factory)*, 1907, gouache on paper, dimensions unknown, private collection. Image courtesy Lynx Theatre and Poetry.

17. *An Old-fashioned Pottery Turning Jasper Ware*, 1907, gouache on paper, 71 × 53.5 cm, private collection. Image courtesy Lynx Theatre and Poetry.

18. *In a Glasgow Cotton Spinning Mill: Changing the Bobbin*, 1907, gouache on paper, 59 × 43.8 cm, private collection. Image courtesy Scarborough Museums Trust.

19. *Old Fashioned Pottery: Transferring the pattern onto the biscuit*, 1907, bodycolour, 51.1 × 33.6 cm, Parliamentary Art Collection. Image © Parliamentary Art Collection, WOA 5922. www.parliament.uk/art.

20. *Scotch Fisher Lassie Cutting Herrings*, 1907, gouache on paper, 59 × 43.8 cm, private collection. Image courtesy Scarborough Museums Trust.

21. *Dipping and Drying on the Mangle*, 1907, charcoal and gouache on paper, 59 × 43.8 cm, private collection. Image courtesy Lynx Theatre and Poetry.

22. HM Williamson & Sons, WSPU tea set, *c*.1909, various dimensions, bone china with printed transfers, Museum of London. Image © Museum of London.

23. Misses MA and E. Brice, West Ham WSPU Banner replicating trumpeting angel motif, 1909–10, cotton, silk, metal and card, H: 105 cm; L: 178 cm, Museum of London. Image © Museum of London.

24. Illuminated Scroll Presented to Holloway Prisoners by the WSPU, *c*.1909, print on paper, 48 × 32 cm, Museum of London. Image © Museum of London.

25. WSPU calendar, 1910, print on card, dimensions unknown, Museum of London. Image © Museum of London.

26. WSPU badge, 1908, tin badge, dimensions unknown, Museum of London. Image © Museum of London.

27. Angel of Freedom emblem, 1908, print on paper, dimensions unknown, Museum of London. Image © Museum of London.

28. Christina Broom, WSPU *Women's Exhibition* featuring Sylvia Pankhurst's decorative mural scheme, 1909, glassplate photograph ½ plate, Museum of London. Image © Museum of London.

29. WSPU *Women's Exhibition* featuring Sylvia Pankhurst's decorative mural scheme, 1909, photograph ½ plate, Pankhurst collection, International Institute of Social History (Amsterdam).

About the author

Katy Norris is a postgraduate researcher, working in partnership with Tate and Bristol University on a Collaborative Doctoral Award, focusing on Edwardian women artists. She previously held the position of Curator at Pallant House Gallery, a leading museum of modern art in the UK. She read History of Art at the University of Warwick and the Courtauld Institute of Art and has curated exhibitions on various themes in Modern British Art. Her publications include *Sickert in Dieppe* (2015) and *Christopher Wood* (2016).

Acknowledgements

I am indebted to Helen Pankhurst who has supported this project from the outset and has generously accommodated the publisher and I in order to bring this book about the life and work of her great-grandmother to fruition. I would like to thank William Alderson, Artistic Director of Lynx Theatre and Poetry who has provided several important images of Sylvia's work and continues to support her legacy. My thanks also to Simon Hedges, Creative Director of Scarborough Museums Trust for sharing images of works featured in the important touring exhibition of Sylvia's work in 2018. Richard Dabb at the Museum of London, Ed Kool at the International Institute of Social History (Amsterdam) and staff at the National Portrait Gallery, London are thanked for their assistance with images also. I am grateful to my PhD Supervisor Emma Chambers for suggesting Sylvia's work as a subject for doctoral research. Finally, I dedicate this book to Tom and Robin.

Index

Sylvia Pankhurst
by Katy Norris
First Edition

First published in the United Kingdom in 2019 by Eiderdown Books
eiderdownbooks.com

Series conceived and developed by Eiderdown Books.
Text copyright © Katy Norris and Eiderdown Books, 2019
Unless otherwise stated, all images copyright © Helen Pankhurst

A CIP catalogue record for this book is available from the British Library

ISBN: 978-1-9160416-0-8

Series Editor: Katy Norris
Editor: Rebeka Cohen
Indexer: Hilary Bird
Series design by Clare Skeats
Typeset by Nicky Barneby in Lelo by Katharina Köhler

The Modern Women Artists logotype is set in Hesse Antiqua,
which was released in 2018 to mark the 100th birthday of
Gudrun Zapf von Hesse. The forms of Hesse Antiqua are based
on the metal punches that von Hesse created in 1947, while working
as a bookbinder at the Bauer Type Foundry in Frankfurt.

Printed and bound by Imago
Reprographics by ALTA